SPY
UNIVERSITY

The Spy's Guide to Secret Codes and Ciphers

BY **Jim Wiese** WITH **H. Keith Melton**
SPY EXPERT

SCHOLASTIC INC.

NEW YORK TORONTO LONDON AUCKLAND SYDNEY
MEXICO CITY NEW DELHI HONG KONG BUENOS AIRES

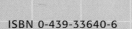

ISBN 0-439-33640-6

Copyright © 2002 by Scholastic Inc.

Editor: Andrea Menotti

Designer: Lee Kaplan   Illustrations: Daniel Aycock

12 11 10 9 8   5 6 7 / 0

Printed in the U.S.A.

First Scholastic printing, October 2002

The publisher has made every effort to ensure that the activities in this book are safe when done as instructed.
Children are encouraged to do their spy activities with willing friends and family members and to respect others'
right to privacy. Adults should provide guidance and supervision whenever the activity requires.

TABLE OF Contents

👀 This means you'll use your Spy Gear in this activity.

💻 This means you can find a related activity on the Spy University web site.

LOADS OF

Check out The Answer Spot on page 48 for hints on these codes.

I f you received a message from another spy-in-training that said ESUOY HT ML AOOHCR SETFE AT MEEM, would you know what to do?

If your Spy University instructor wrote ATYAHHAJP on your progress report, would you want to hang it up proudly on the refrigerator, or would you wonder what went wrong? Not sure?

Well, that's why you've got this new guide, so let's get cracking!

This month, you'll learn the kinds of **codes** and **ciphers** that spies use to keep their messages from being read by the wrong people. We've got lots of them here, so learn them all and pick your favorites. Then you can use them to write messages that'll only be understood by the people you choose.

But before you jump in, let's answer a few basic questions:

> ESUOY HT ML AOOHCR SETFE AT MEEM

SPY UNIVERSITY

Progress Report

Ima Spy
name

ATYAHHAJP!

JUST WHAT IS A CODE, EXACTLY?

A code is a secret language that a certain group of people agree to use when they communicate with each other. It's a way of hiding the meaning of a message by using a system of letters, numbers, words, symbols, sounds, or signals to represent the actual text of the message. So, when a message is **encoded** (or put into code), the plain old words of the message are hidden safely away, and the message can't be understood unless you know the **message key** (that's the secret set of rules the code system follows). Once you know the message key, you can **decode** the message (that is, you can change it back into plain old words).

For example, there's a famous code from the American Revolutionary War (1775–1783) in which two lanterns hanging in a church steeple were used to communicate information to the American colonists. The rules of the code were simple (and they're famous now): "One if by land,

"One if by land, and two if by sea."

4

CODES!

and two if by sea." If *one* lantern was lit, the colonists knew that the British were invading by land. If *two* lanterns were lit, then the British were coming by sea. This code used symbols (the two lanterns) whose secret meaning was agreed upon by the colonists beforehand.

OKAY, THEN WHAT'S A CIPHER?

A cipher is a special type of code that only uses letters or numbers (not symbols or signals or anything like that). When a message is **enciphered**, the real letters of the message are replaced by a new set of letters or numbers. It's a letter-for-letter substitution (or a number-for-letter substitution). For example, the word "apple" could be written 1-16-16-12-5 as a cipher. In this cipher, each letter in the word has been replaced by a number. The number comes from the order of the letter in the alphabet (A=1, B=2, C=3, and so on).

You already know the Caesar cipher from your *Trainee Handbook*. In that cipher, the real letters of a message are swapped with a new set of letters that has been created by shifting the alphabet a few letters over (for example, in a three-letter shift, A is replaced by D, B is replaced by E, C by F, and so on). As this book will show you, there are plenty more ciphers that are a lot tougher to crack (or **decipher**) than that one!

WHO USES CODES?

Spies aren't the only ones who send and receive messages in code. Codes are also used by the military to communicate information and commands. In times of war, the work of **cryptologists** (experts in making and breaking codes) is enormously important. Breaking a code can change the whole course of a war, as you'll see when you read this month's Spy Feature!

Codes are used in plenty of other situations as well. Sports teams use code systems to secretly share strategies on the field, and banks use them to keep financial information private and secure.

Hospitals also use codes to alert doctors and nurses when emergencies arise. Code blue, for example, means that someone's having a heart attack, code red means there's a fire, and so on. This way, when the code is announced, the people who are supposed to respond know immediately what to do, and outsiders (like patients and visitors) don't have to know what's going on.

To sum it all up, codes are used by anyone who has information that needs to be wrapped up in special packaging when it's sent out into the world. For spies, the packaging has to be so tough and so cleverly crafted that only the people who are supposed to receive the information will know how to open it. That's the challenge that cryptologists face, and that's your challenge, too, as you start your training in secret codes and ciphers. What kinds of codes can you trust? What kinds of codes can you create? Read on, and find out!

ABOUT THIS MONTH'S SPY GEAR

 This month, you've been issued a pair of **Morse code** transmitters. Have an adult help you install 9-volt batteries, then try your hand at **Operation Morse of Course** on page 10, where you'll learn how to use your transmitters to turn a message into a series of short and long beeps (otherwise known as **dots and dashes**). These are not walkie-talkies, by the way—so they're not for transmitting voice communications (since Morse is the spy's choice, of course)!

ABOUT THIS MONTH'S WEB SITE

You now have access to a whole new on-line training session at the Spy University web site at **www.scholastic.com/spy**. It's got all kinds of code-making and code-breaking machines, including one that'll play your messages in Morse code. So grab your new password and get on-line!

the **password** spot

This month's web site password:

catchacode

Here are this month's spy terms. Get to know them! And whenever you see a word in **bold** throughout the book, you can always turn back to this page to refresh your memory.

▼ **Cipher:** A form of code in which the letters of a message are replaced with a new set of letters or numbers according to some rule.

▼ **Cipher table:** A table of letters used to create ciphers.

▼ **Cipher wheel:** A device that uses disks (with letters on them) to create ciphers.

▼ **Classified information:** Information available to a limited number of people.

▼ **Code:** A system designed to hide the meaning of a message by using letters, numbers, words, symbols, sounds, or signals to represent the actual text.

▼ **Cryptology:** The study of hidden, disguised, or encoded communications (a **cryptologist** is an expert in this field).

▼ **Decipher:** To take a message out of cipher form and put it into plain text.

▼ **Decode:** To take a message out of code form and put it into plain text.

▼ **Dots and dashes:** The short and long signals used in Morse code.

▼ **Double encrypting:** Taking a message that's already in code or cipher, and encrypting it again with another system.

▼ **Encipher:** To put a message in cipher.

▼ **Encode:** To put a message in code.

▼ **Encrypt:** Another word for putting a message into code or cipher.

▼ **Key word:** A word that's used as the basis for creating a cipher (see **Operation Cipher Table** and **Operation Spy Code**).

▼ **Message key:** The set of rules used for a code or cipher system.

▼ **Morse code:** A code that assigns each letter a pattern of short and long signals according to a system established internationally in 1851.

▼ **Spy network:** A group of spies who work together toward a common goal.

This cipher reel was used by the Confederate army during the American Civil War (1861–1865). The principal cipher system the Confederates used was the Vigenere system, which involved a cipher table (turn to page 34 to learn all about this). This cipher reel made it easier to read the cipher table.

THE CASE OF THE Writing

ON THE CHALKBOARD

It's Monday morning, and you get to school a bit early. None of your friends have arrived yet, so you decide to go inside and sit beside your classroom door to wait for everyone. You sit there for about five minutes before your teacher, Ms. Lightly, arrives.

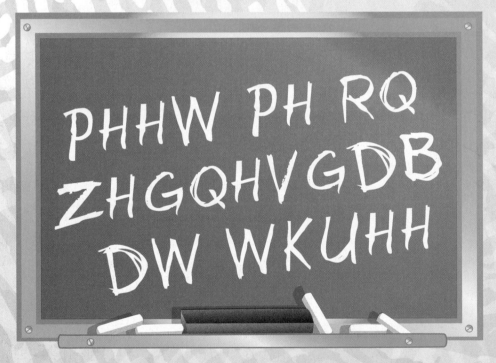

She greets you and unlocks the door, and you enter the classroom together. Ms. Lightly is a really good teacher, and you like her a lot.

"How'd you do on your math homework this weekend?" Ms. Lightly asks.

"Okay," you say. "But there was one problem I couldn't get."

"Put it on the chalkboard," she says. "We'll have a look at it together."

As you head toward the front of the room, you notice that there's some strange writing on the chalkboard. It's right smack in the middle of the board, and it reads: **PHHW PH RQ ZHGQHVGDB DW WKUHH**.

"Ms. Lightly," you say. "What's this?"

Ms. Lightly turns to see the writing on the board, and she looks surprised for a moment before she catches herself.

"I don't know," she shrugs. "Just erase it, please."

"It looks like some kind of code," you say. "Doesn't it?"

"Whatever it is, it doesn't belong up there," Ms. Lightly says. "Could you erase it for me, please?"

There's something in the tone of her voice that makes you think she knows more about this than she's admitting. As you reach for the eraser, you wonder if you should copy down the letters before you erase them. Then maybe you could try to figure out the code….

But then again, you wonder if it's even worth making the effort. This might just be the work of some kids playing around after school. You wonder if you should ask Ms. Lightly a few more questions to get a better idea of who might have written those letters.

■ If you decide to copy down the letters so you can decode them later, turn to **page 32**.

■ If you decide to question Ms. Lightly, turn to **page 28**.

This is your Spy Quest for this month. There's only one way to solve it, so choose your path wisely! If you hit a dead end, you'll have to back up and choose another path!

1

OPERATION Morse of course

Ever heard of **Morse code**? It sounds like this: "Beep beep beep. Beeeeeep beeeeeep beeeeeep. Beep beep beep." (That's three short beeps, three long beeps, and three short beeps.) In Morse code, each letter gets its own pattern of short and long beeps—or if not beeps, then any kind of signal that can be heard or seen. The short signals are called **dots** (.), and the long signals are called **dashes** (–). Use the chart on the next page to see what the beeps in the example above spell out. (And if you need *help* on that, check out **What's the Secret?** on page 13.)

Secret? on page 13.

STUFF YOU'LL NEED

- 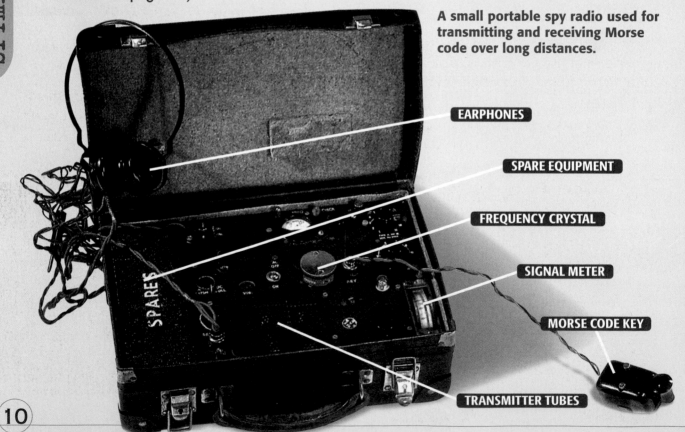 Morse code transmitters
- Pencil and paper

YOUR NETWORK

- A friend to receive your transmissions

SPYmissions

A small portable spy radio used for transmitting and receiving Morse code over long distances.

EARPHONES

SPARE EQUIPMENT

FREQUENCY CRYSTAL

SIGNAL METER

MORSE CODE KEY

TRANSMITTER TUBES

Spies like Morse code because it can be transmitted and received by radio over long distances more clearly than voice signals. Also, it's easier to **encipher** Morse code messages than to "scramble" voice messages so they can't be understood.

On this page, you can see an example of a Morse code radio. A spy would use a portable instrument like this to send Morse code from the field back to headquarters. Your transmitters are the portable kind, too.

So, let's power up your transmitters and start sending some code! Once you've learned the basics (and heard enough beeps), you can move on to **Operation Quiet Morse** (coming up next) and try other ways of sending Morse code that don't require any sound at all!

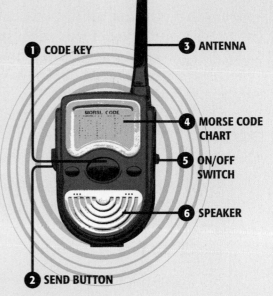

1 CODE KEY
3 ANTENNA
4 MORSE CODE CHART
5 ON/OFF SWITCH
6 SPEAKER
2 SEND BUTTON

WHAT YOU DO

1 Think of a message that you want to send to your friend. Your first message should be a simple one, like: "I know my Morse." That's positive thinking—always a good thing!

2 Study the chart below to get acquainted with Morse code. Each letter in the alphabet and each numeral has its own series of dots and dashes. For example, the letter A is **. –** (pronounced "dot, dash"), and the letter B is **– . . .** (pronounced "dash, dot, dot, dot").

3 In addition to the signals for the letters and numbers, you (and your friend) will also need to know the sender's and receiver's signals. Here they are:

MORSE CODE

A • –	M – –	Y – • – –
B – • • •	N – •	Z – – • •
C – • – •	O – – –	1 • – – – –
D – • •	P • – – •	2 • • – – –
E •	Q – – • –	3 • • • – –
F • • – •	R • – •	4 • • • • –
G – – •	S • • •	5 • • • • •
H • • • •	T –	6 – • • • •
I • •	U • • –	7 – – • • •
J • – – –	V • • • –	8 – – – • •
K – • –	W • – –	9 – – – – •
L • – • •	X – • • –	0 – – – – –

	MORSE CODE	MEANING
SENDER'S SIGNALS:	• – • –	About to send signal.
	• • • –	End of message.
RECEIVER'S SIGNALS:	• –	Ready to receive. (At the end of message, it means "message understood.")
	• • • • • •	Not ready to receive. (At the end of a message, it means "not understood.")

4 Make sure that your transmitters are turned on, and give one to your friend, along with the pencil and paper. He should then move somewhere else, up to 100 yards (100 meters) away from you, but no more. It's best if you're outside, but if you're inside, have your friend go to the next room. (You can even close the door, and the signals should still get through.)

5 When your friend is in position, hold down your transmitter's send button with your left

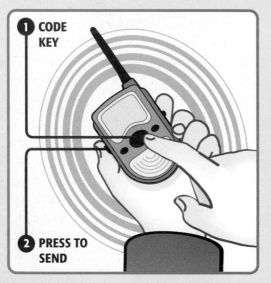

1 CODE KEY

2 PRESS TO SEND

thumb, and press the code key with your right index finger to transmit the sender's signal (**. — . —**). Press the code key down for one second for a dot and two seconds for a dash.

6 Release the send button and wait till you hear the receiver's signal (**. –**), so you know it's okay to send your message.

BEEP BEEEEP

7 Send your message in Morse code. Again, hold down the send button and press the code key for one second for a dot and two seconds for a dash.

8 Put a short pause between each letter and a long pause between each word.

9 Your friend can **decode** the message by turning the dots and dashes you sent back into the letters they stand for. He should write down the letters as they come through. (That's why he needs the pencil and paper!)

10 At the end of your message, tack on the "end of message" signal (**. . . –**).

11 Wait for the receiver's signal to tell you that the message was understood (**. –**). If you hear that, then you and your friend definitely know your Morse! If you hear this (**. . . . . .**), you'd better try again!

SPYquest

(continued from page 32)

You wait around in your classroom after school. Ms. Lightly helps a few students with their math problems and then tells everyone that she has to go. You all pick up your books and leave. You wait down the hall, around the corner, and watch as Ms. Lightly locks the classroom door. She stands in the hallway, looking in both directions.

As you peek around the corner for a better look, you're startled by a voice behind you.

"Looking for something?"

You quickly turn around and bump into Mr. Shader, your science teacher.

"Are you supposed to be in school this late?" he asks.

You come up with an excuse about waiting for a friend, but you can tell he doesn't buy it. He tells you it's time to leave.

You do as he says. Now what can you do?

■ If you decide to come to school early tomorrow to look for more clues, turn to **page 30**.

■ If you decide to go outside and wait for Ms. Lightly to come out of the building, turn to **page 25**.

MORE FROM HEADQUARTERS

1 Receive a message in Morse code on your transmitter! Switch roles with your friend and practice your decoding skills.

2 Stop by the Spy University web site at **www.scholastic.com/spy**, and you can type in a message and hear it played in Morse code. You can also listen to some sample transmissions to get more practice at receiving and decoding Morse messages.

3 Try sending an enciphered message using Morse code. See **Operation ADFGX Cipher** on page 26 for a great example of a cipher that's easy to transmit in Morse code.

WHAT'S THE SECRET?

The coded message in the introduction stands for "SOS." That means *help!* It's known all over the world as the Universal Distress Signal. The letters SOS don't really stand for anything, but they'll be easy to remember if you think of them as meaning "Save Our Ship." They were chosen because they're very easy to send and understand in Morse code. Try it yourself and you'll see.

Your Morse code transmitters send their signals using radio waves. Those are the same waves that send music to your radio, but the waves made by your transmitters have more limited power and range. Some spy radios (like the one shown on page 10) can send and receive Morse code signals over much greater distances than AM or FM radio signals can carry.

A Morse code radio operator sending signals.

SPYtales

Morse code was invented by Samuel Morse in 1844. Morse also invented a machine called a telegraph to send his codes. To use Morse's telegraph, operators at one end pressed a key to send signals. Pressing the key closed the electric circuit, allowing electricity to flow. The electricity traveled across wires to the recipient's end, where it activated either a clicker (which clicked out long or short sounds that were recorded as dots or dashes), or an inker (which actually printed out the dots and dashes). The dots and dashes were then translated into words using Morse code. This new technology meant that messages could be sent across great distances. In fact, during the American Civil War (1861–1865), telegraph signals were used to send orders to armies (in cipher).

But the telegraph had one big drawback: It needed a direct wire link between both ends, so messages could only be sent to and from certain locations. A breakthrough came in 1888, when German scientist Heinrich Hertz discovered radio waves. Seven years later, an Italian named Guglielmo Marconi made the first successful radio transmission. From then on, spies had a much better way of sending messages, without the limits of wires.

OPERATION Quiet MORSE

#2

Morse code can also be sent without a peep (or a beep or a click)! Visual signals like flashes of light and winks of the eye can transmit the code, too. You'll need to know your Morse signals pretty well to handle these operations, so go back and review the chart on page 11. Then try these two techniques, and see how there's more to Morse than meets the *ear*!

STUFF YOU'LL NEED
- **Two flashlights**
- **Pencil and paper**

YOUR NETWORK
- **A senior spy (an adult) to join you in Part 1**
- **A friend to receive your message in Part 2**

WHAT YOU DO

PART 1: DOT AND DASH IN A FLASH

Suppose you need a way to send a senior spy some information during a night operation and you don't have your Morse code transmitters. If he's far away from you, what can you do? Try this!

1 Plan a message that you want to send to the senior spy. Choose a simple message, such as: "Move west."

2 Go outside on a dark night, and have the senior spy stand at least 50 yards (50 meters) away from you.

3 Turn the flashlight on, then cover the lens with your hand.

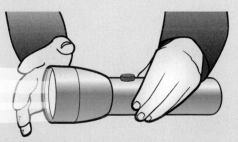

4 Now send your message in Morse code. Uncover the flashlight for one second for a dot and two seconds for a dash.

5 Use a three-second pause between each letter and a six-second pause to mark the end of a word.

6 The senior spy can translate the flashes back into letters. He should write down the letters as he receives them (using his own flashlight to see).

PART 2: WINKIN', BLINKIN', AND NOD

If you're in a situation where talking isn't an option, but your friend can easily see your face (like when you're sitting across from each other in class), you can send Morse code in the blink of an eye!

1 Decide on a message that you want to send to your friend. Choose a simple message like: "Keep quiet."

2 Your friend should be sitting across the room from you.

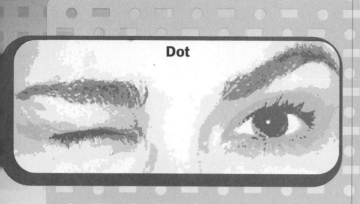

Dot

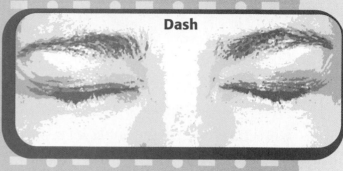

Dash

3 Now use eye blinks to send your message in Morse code. A single blink of your right eye is a dot, and a blink of both eyes is a dash.

4 Use a short pause at the end of each letter, and a longer pause to indicate the end of a word.

5 Your friend will translate the coded message back into letters. As always, writing down the letters will help.

MORE FROM HEADQUARTERS

Here's what Morse code looks like on paper. To make decoding easier, a slash (/) signifies the end of a letter and two slashes (//) indicate the end of a word. Three slashes (///) indicate the end of a sentence. Practice your Morse code skills by decoding the following dots and dashes. You'll find the answer on page 48.

– /. . . . /. // – – /. . / . . . / . . . /. . / – – – /
– . // . . . / – / . – /. – . / – / . . . //
– – –/ – . // – – /– – – / – . / – . . /
. – / – . – – ///

WHAT'S THE SECRET?

When you don't have a Morse code radio transmitter available, light signals like the ones you made with your flashlight can travel a long distance. They're useful for ships at sea in emergency situations.

Eye blink signals like the ones you learned in Part 2 can be done very unnoticeably. The technique was actually used by American prisoners during the Vietnam War (in the 1960s and 70s). They sent secret messages home by using eye blinks when they were being filmed by their captors.

(continued from page 25 or 41)

When you get home, you compare the messages you've found so far. The one thing that's missing from the first message (the one on the chalkboard) is the place where the meeting will happen. Is it possible that "starlight" is the name of a place?

You go grab the phone book and look up "starlight." In fact, there's a Starlight Cinema and a Starlight Café. Maybe one of these is the meeting place? But which one? You can't be in both places at once!

You look on a map, and you find that it would take you at least half an hour by bike to reach either of the two places from school. It'll be tough to get to either one by 3:00, since school gets out at 2:30!

■ If you decide to go to the Starlight Cinema, turn to **page 38**.

■ If you decide to go to the Starlight Café, turn to **page 47**.

15

3

OPERATION
cipherwheel

Remember the Caesar cipher from your *Trainee Handbook*? That **cipher** used a simple letter substitution to create a secret message. You put one alphabet underneath another, sliding the lower one over a few spots to get your cipher. Well, to make your work easier, now you're going to make something called a **cipher wheel** that you can use to create twenty-five different types of Caesar ciphers!

STUFF YOU'LL NEED

- **Pencil and paper**
- **Marker**
- **Scissors**
- **Paper clip**
- **Paper fastener (optional)**

ABCDEFGHIJKLMNOPQRSTUVWXYZ
EFGHIJKLMNOPQRSTUVWXYZABCD

WHAT YOU DO

1 Using your pencil, trace the two disks on page 17 onto a piece of paper. Trace every line on the disks, including the spaces for the letters. Then go over your tracing with a marker, to make it bolder. If you don't like tracing, see **More from Headquarters** for instructions on how to do this with your computer and printer.

2 Print the alphabet, one letter in each space, on both disks.

3 Carefully cut out the disks.

4 Place the inner circle on top of the outer circle.

5 Choose your cipher by moving the inner disk around until the letter you want lines up with the A on the outer disk. In our example, we've chosen to shift the alphabet four letters, so A lines up with E.

Use a paper clip to hold the two disks in place until you want to change the cipher. Place the paper clip over the A and the letter you've chosen.

6 If you have a paper fastener (sometimes called a "brad"), you can use that to attach the inner disk to the outer disk. Just push it through the middle of the two disks, then bend out the tabs underneath the disks. You should still use a paper clip to mark your cipher.

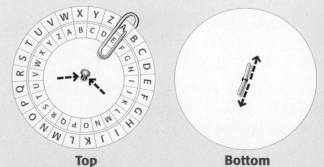

Top   **Bottom**

7 Now you're ready to **encipher** a message! Just follow the usual Caesar cipher process. Find the letter you want to encipher on the outer wheel and look below it (on the inner wheel) to find the cipher letter. To **decipher** a message, do the reverse.

ACTUAL LETTER

CIPHER LETTER

8 Have the friend who receives your messages make a cipher wheel, too. Or, if you want, make one for your friend as a gift, from spy to spy.

MORE FROM HEADQUARTERS

1 Go to the Spy University web site (**www.scholastic.com/spy**) and print out the cipher wheel, if you don't want to trace it. Then just cut it out and assemble it! This is an easy way to make lots of cipher wheels to share with your **spy network**.

2 Try enciphering the following plain text messages using a cipher that shifts the second alphabet five letters clockwise (so A lines up with F). You can check your answers by turning to page 48.

   a. Beware of Paula. I think she's listening to us.

   b. Meet me at Checkpoint Alpha.

3 Decipher the messages on the next page. They all use the same **message key**, so see if you can figure them out by trying a few options.

Outer disk (above) and inner disk (below) to trace.

Notice that there are some one-letter words. What could those letters be? Make a guess, then use your cipher wheel to line up the cipher letter (on the inner wheel) with the letter you think it represents (on the outer wheel). Can you decipher the rest of the message using that message key? If you can, then you've found the right one. You can check your answers on page 48.

- a. **YD NDAIZ UE ZAF DQMXXK ITA TQ EMKE TQ UE**
- b. **IQMD M PUESGUEQ FA FTQ YQQFUZS**
- c. **U IUXX IQMD M DQP TMF EA KAG IUXX DQOASZULQ YQ**

WHAT'S THE SECRET?

If you had to write out two whole alphabets, one on top of the other, whenever you wanted to encipher or decipher a message, it would take a long time. That's what makes your cipher wheel really handy! It allows you to try out lots of different message keys very quickly.

(continued from page 32)

You wait outside the classroom on Wednesday afternoon. Sure enough, at 2:45, Ms. Lightly rushes out. You follow her, thinking she's planned her meeting somewhere in the school building.

But you're wrong.

She goes right to the parking lot, gets in her car, and drives off. Soon she's out of sight.

You have no idea where she might have gone. Too bad you don't have more information!

■ This was a dead end. Go back and try again!

The cipher wheel, or cipher disk, is said to have been invented by the Italian scholar Leon Battista Alberti in the fifteenth century. Alberti was an architect, painter, writer, and composer. And, if these weren't enough, he also had code-breaking talents. Alberti applied his genius to helping the Pope decipher secret messages he received. By using his cipher disk, Alberti could easily test lots of different ways of deciphering the messages. In 1466, Alberti wrote the first known text on cryptology, the study of secret codes and ciphers.

This cipher disk was used by the Confederate army Secret Signal Corps during the American Civil War (1861–1865).

OPERATION DEEPER meaning

Simple notes and letters to friends may look ordinary and unsuspicious, but in the spy world, things are not always what they seem. You've got to read between the lines! With a **code** system in place, a secret message can hide in an innocent, friendly note. Try this activity to see how.

STUFF YOU'LL NEED
● **Pencil and paper**

YOUR NETWORK
● **A friend to receive your hidden message**

WHAT YOU DO

PART 1: BON VOYAGE

1 Suppose you received the following letter from your friend. You know that a secret message is hidden in it. Can you figure it out?

> Dear Liz,
>
> You really surprised me with your last letter. Will you really get to do what you said? Meet a movie star! A person like you sure is lucky. New York will be great this time of year. Contact Jeff for me while you're there and say hello. Tomorrow I'll be thinking of you on your flight. At noon, I'll look for your plane and wave as you fly overhead. Four more weeks till I get to see you!
>
> -J.W.

2 To **decode** the hidden message, use the pencil and paper to write down the first word in each sentence (not counting the greeting). What is the secret message? You can check if you're right by turning to page 48.

PART 2: PEN PAL

1 Read the letter below. Another secret message is hidden in it. Can you see it?

> Dear Michael,
>
> Jack, Thomas and I all say hi! Jenny's family moved into the country, but she's not happy about it. Heard from Sarah. Each time I hear from her she's changed schools. Not fun! I'm in the same old school. My studies started slowly. Teachers are okay, and so are the other students. About two weeks ago things got better. I turned in my book report on Harriet the Spy then. I'd be lying if I didn't tell you that it's one of the best papers I've ever written. Mr. Lang, my English teacher, is awesome. In graphics and art classes I'm doing well. I better end now. My neighbor wants me to mow his lawn. Catch you later.
>
> -J

2 To decode the hidden message, use your pencil and paper to write down the third letter

19

in the first word (not counting the greeting) and then the third letter after every punctuation mark—that is, all the periods (**.**), commas (**,**), and exclamation points (**!**).

3 Separate the letters into words to read the secret message. You can check if you're right by turning to page 48.

4 Now use either of these forms of hidden writing to send a message to a friend. Try something easy, like: "Meet me after school." Make sure your friend knows in advance what the **message key** is. Otherwise, the letter really *is* just an ordinary letter!

This postcard was sent to the FBI by an American prisoner of war in Japan during World War II. This code is known as a "null code," and you can read it by eliminating all but the first two words in each line: "AFTER SURRENDER, FIFTY PERCENT AMERICANS LOST IN PHILIPPINES. IN NIPPON 30 PERCENT." Notice also how cleverly the writer has disguised the fact that he's writing to the FBI!

MORE FROM HEADQUARTERS

1 Try different ways of hiding a secret message in a letter. You could use the second word in each sentence, or the first or second letter after every punctuation mark to make up your secret message. You could also use the first and last letters in each sentence. Be creative!

2 Now that you've become creative with your code, come up with a clever way to let your friend know what the message key is. You could use invisible ink (like you learned in your *Trainee Handbook*) to tell your friend the message key, or you could agree on a system in advance that would allow you to plant the message key information right in the letter. For example, if you ended the letter with "See you later," that could tell your friend to use the first word in each sentence. If you ended the letter with "Keep in touch," that could tell your friend to use the third letter after each punctuation mark.

FRANK G. JONELIS, 1st Lt. USA
ZENTSUJI WAR PRISONERS CAMP
NIPPON

MR. F.B. IERS
% FEDERAL BLDG. COMPANY
ROOM 1619. 100 MNN ST.
LOS ANGELES CALIFORNIA
U.S.A.
CENSORED
EXAMINED
P 627

AUGUST 29, 1943

DEAR IERS:
AFTER SURRENDER, HEALTH IMPROVED
FIFTY PERCENT. BETTER FOOD ETC.
AMERICANS LOST CONFIDENCE
IN PHILIPPINES. AM COMFORTABLE
IN NIPPON. MOTHER: INVEST
30%, SALARY, IN BUSINESS. LOVE

Frank G. Jonelis

WHAT'S THE SECRET?

This type of code writing is difficult because you have to place specific words in each sentence to spell out your message. It can be very hard to spell out the message and make the letter sound natural at the same time. It's worth the effort, though, because this type of code is tough to break! If the letter is well written, an enemy spy may not realize it contains a secret message. And even if the spy *does* suspect there's a hidden message, it'll be tough to figure it out because the possible message keys are endless!

(*continued from page 25 or 41*)

You follow Ms. Lightly out of the school building at 2:45. She goes right to the parking lot, gets in her car, and drives off. Soon she's out of sight. Even though you have your bike on hand, there's no way you could follow on the bike path and keep her in view. Where in the world did she go? That mysterious word "starlight" keeps nagging you. If only you'd figured out what it meant! That might have helped you prepare.

■ It looks like you've hit a dead end. Go back and try again!

In seventeenth-century England, Oliver Cromwell, a religious and political leader, overthrew King Charles I and ruled the country for a brief time. During Cromwell's reign, many people remained loyal to the king. They were called Royalists, and they were imprisoned if caught. One of the captured Royalists was Sir John Trevanion.

Royalists like Trevanion were usually put in prison and often executed for treason (that is, attempting to betray or overthrow the government). However, several days before his execution, Trevanion received a letter from his servant, which is shown on the right.

Can you decode the secret message in the letter? It says: "Panel at east end of chapel slides." Now can you figure it out? It uses the secret code from Part 2 of this operation, in which the third letter after every punctuation mark forms a word.

Trevanion read the letter, then requested a private hour inside the prison chapel. But rather than spending the time in prayer, he escaped out the false panel in the chapel that he had learned about in the letter!

Worthy Sir John:

Hope, that is ye best comfort of ye afflicted, cannot much, I fear me, help you now. That I would say to you, is this only: if ever I may be able to requite that I do owe you, stand not upon asking me. Tis not much that I can do: but what I can do, bee ye very sure I will. I know that, if death comes, if ordinary men fear it, it frights not you, accounting it for a high honour, to have such a reward of your loyalty. Pray yet that you may be spared this so bitter, cup. I fear not that you will grudge any sufferings; only if the submission you can turn them away, tis the part of a wise man. Tell me, as if you can, to do for you anything that you would have done. The general goes back on Wednesday. Resting is your servant to command.

— R.E.

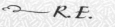

double talk

A spoken **code** can turn an ordinary conversation into a hiding place for secrets. In a spoken (or "verbal") code, the words you say have another meaning that you've arranged beforehand. For example, if a spy asks his handler, "How's your day been? Busy?" it might mean, "How is our security? Have we been exposed?"

STUFF YOU'LL NEED
● **Pencil and paper**
● **Telephone**

YOUR NETWORK
● **A friend to communicate with**

You can choose any code words or phrases you want for your spoken code. Your job, though, is to try to make the conversation still seem ordinary, so no one overhearing it will get suspicious. See how spies can develop their own secret vocabularies by giving this operation a try.

WHAT YOU DO

1 Work with your friend to develop a code that can be used on the phone to let you know if it's safe to discuss **classified information** (that is, top secret stuff that you don't want anyone else to overhear). This code should be really simple.

For example, if you call and say, "Hi, how are you?" your friend can reply in two ways. If he says, "I'm fine. How are you?" that could mean that it's safe to discuss classified information, since there's no one around to overhear. If he says, "Everything is great. How are you?" then you know that the situation on your friend's end is not secure, and no further classified communication should take place. Since both responses are positive and would lead to more talking, no one overhearing the conversation would suspect that it's unusual in any way.

2 Create a larger set of code words that can be used to talk with your friend. Some examples are listed in the chart on the left.

Using these code words, you could tell a

CODE WORD(S)	MEANING
Dad	**Handler**
Mom	**Headquarters (HQ)**
Do homework	**Keep close watch on someone**
Today	**Tomorrow**
Tomorrow	**Today**
Clean my room	**Send a secret message**
Play a game	**Have a meeting**
Ride my bike	**Follow someone**
After dinner	**After school**

fellow spy, "Mom wants me to clean my room today." Even if someone overhears the conversation, it'll still sound pretty ordinary (especially if your room needs cleaning!). It means: "Headquarters wants me to send a secret message tomorrow."

3 Use your code words to communicate by phone with your friend.

Hi, how are you?

Everything is great. How are you?

MORE FROM HEADQUARTERS

Translate these coded messages using the chart on page 22. Check your answers on page 48.

a. I'm going to ride my bike tomorrow.

b. Let's play a game after dinner today.

WHAT'S THE SECRET?

When you create your own vocabulary, you have to choose words and phrases that will be easy for you and your friend to remember. Keep it simple!

SPYtales

During World War II (1939–1945), the U.S. Marines fighting in the Pacific transmitted their messages without encoding them. They didn't need codes; they used Navajo Code Talkers instead.

The Navajo are Native Americans who live in the Southwest United States. Their language is unwritten (with no alphabet or symbols), and it's extremely difficult to learn without a lot of training. Not many people know the language outside of the Navajo population.

The idea for the Navajo Code Talkers came from Philip Johnston, one of the few non-Navajos who spoke the Navajo language. Johnston knew that Navajo was the perfect language to use in radio communications because it was so little known.

In May 1942, the first Navajo recruits attended boot camp and created the Navajo code, developing a dictionary and numerous words for military terms. They then memorized what they had created and were sent into the field, where they became the Navajo Code Talkers. With a Code Talker on each end of a radio or telephone conversation, the marines knew that their messages would not be understood by the enemy. By 1945, there were over 400 Navajos serving their country in this way.

The Japanese, who were skilled code breakers, were never able to crack the Navajo language code.

Navajo code talkers.

OPERATION PIG PEN CODE

#6

No, you won't have to visit a barnyard for this operation, but you *will* make some lines that look like the fences that go around pigpens. That's where this **code** got its name. Variations of it were used by soldiers in the Civil War as an easy way to get messages past the enemy. Try it, and you'll see how a symbol system can hold a message inside (like a pig in a pen!).

STUFF YOU'LL NEED

- **Pencil and paper**

YOUR NETWORK

- **A friend to receive your messages**

WHAT YOU DO

1 To make the key for the Pigpen code, begin by drawing two tic-tac-toe grids. Then draw two large X shapes beside them, as shown here.

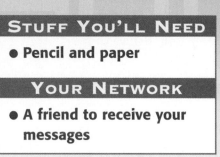

2 In the second tic-tac-toe shape, put a dot in each "pen" (that is, in each space of the grid). Do the same to the second X shape.

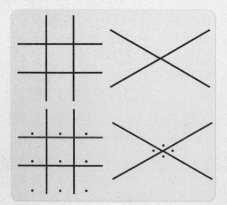

3 Now write a different letter in each of the "pens," as shown on the right.

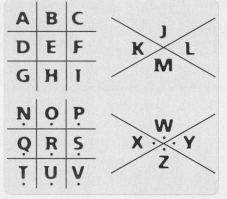

4 The symbol for each letter is the pen that it sits in. So, the symbol may be just lines like for E ☐ , or it might be lines and a dot, like for W ⩒ .

5 Write a message to your friend using the Pigpen code. For example, the word SECRET would be written like this:

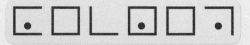

6 Make sure your friend has a copy of the code, and then pass him your Pigpen message. To **decode** it, your friend will simply convert each symbol into the letter it stands for.

7 Have your friend write you back, so you can test your decoding skills!

MORE FROM HEADQUARTERS

1 Practice decoding these Pigpen messages. (You can check your answers on page 48.)

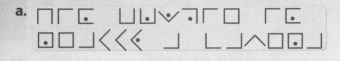

a.

b.

c.

2 There are many variations of the Pigpen code. Try making one of your own. One way is to change the way the letters of the alphabet are arranged in the tic-tac-toe shapes and the X shapes. Remember to keep your letter arrangement simple, and you'll need to create a **message key** so the receiver of your message will be able to decode it.

WHAT'S THE SECRET?

The Pigpen code is really just a substitution code that uses simple shapes and dots to create symbols. It's great because you don't have to worry that you'll forget the symbols. You can just quickly create a message key each time you write or read a message by setting up the tic-tac-toe grids and the X shapes.

The downside of the Pigpen code is that it's pretty well-known, so your messages might be decoded by the wrong people. It's probably best if you have several different ways to arrange the alphabet in the "pens." That'll help keep your messages secret.

(continued from page 12)

You walk outside the school and toward the teachers' parking lot. You recognize Ms. Lightly's little green car immediately. All the kids know it because it's the most brightly colored car in the lot, and also because it has a bumper sticker that says, "If you can read this, thank a teacher."

Then your eye catches something—there's a note under Ms. Lightly's windshield wiper! You quickly move to the car, turning to make sure that Ms. Lightly hasn't come out of the building yet. You grab the note and open it. You see:

Psst. You can check your answer on page 48!

You recognize the Pigpen code immediately, but you don't have time to decode it on the spot. You quickly jot the code down in your notebook, replace the note under the windshield wiper, and head over to the playground to decode the message.

It's pretty easy to decode the message (since the letters were arranged in the pens the usual way), but you're not sure what it means. The last three words make sense, since they fit with what you read on the chalkboard, but the first word makes no sense at all. What do the stars have to do with anything? Is this a weather forecast? Somehow you know it's not that simple.

- If you decide to do some research to figure out what the first word is all about, turn to **page 15**.
- If you decide the best plan is just to wait until Wednesday and follow Ms. Lightly then, turn to **page 21**.

ADFGX CIPHER

#7

You've learned that **Morse code** is a great way to transmit wireless, wordless messages. The code is so well known, though, that an intercepted message would be quickly **decoded**. That's why it's a good idea to **encipher** messages before sending them in Morse code. Using a **cipher** also means that top secret messages can be kept secure even if they're handled by many radio operators.

The ADFGX cipher is perfect for sending in Morse code. Devised by the Germans during World War I, it only uses five letters—A, D, F, G, and X—which are easy to tell apart in Morse code. The German army needed a cipher that was easy to transmit like this, because it had a large number of radio operators, and some of them were poorly trained and tended to make errors when tapping out Morse code signals. With just five letters, the ADFGX cipher meant they had less to worry about!

If you've already done **Operation Morse of Course** on page 10, then you're ready to send and receive messages in the ADFGX cipher. Read on!

STUFF YOU'LL NEED
● **Pencil and paper**
● 👓 **Morse Code transmitters**

YOUR NETWORK
● **A friend to receive your transmissions in Part 2**

WHAT YOU DO

PART 1: LEARN THE CIPHER

1 The ADFGX cipher is based on a five-by-five grid. That means that the five letters A, D, F, G, and X make up the top row and the left side of a checkerboard arrangement, as shown here.

	A	D	F	G	X
A	n	b	x	r	u
D	q	o	k	d	v
F	a	h	s	g	f
G	m	z	c	l	t
X	e	i	p	j	w

The letters of the alphabet go inside the spaces in the checkerboard.

2 Each letter in a message is enciphered with a pair of letters. The letter K, for example, would be enciphered DF. To see how this works, find the letter K inside the grid. Then look at the far left side column and find the letter that's directly across from the K (that's D). For the second letter, look at the top row and take the letter that's directly above the K (that's F). For every letter, you go through the same process. The letter from the left column is the first letter, and the letter from the top row is the second letter. When you encipher a whole message, leave a space between each pair of letters.

3 How would you encipher the word "secret"? Try it, and check your answer on page 48.

4 To **decipher** a message that's in the ADFGX cipher, simply reverse the process. For GF, for example, look across the G row until you find the letter that's underneath the F (that's C). Try deciphering the word **GF DD DG XA**. You already have the first letter, so finish up the other three and check your answer on page 48.

5 If you intercepted this message, could you decipher it? Check your answer on page 48.

GA XA XA GX   FA GX   DG FA XX AA

PART 2: TRANSMISSION TIME

A	• —
D	— • •
F	• • — •
G	— — •
X	— • • —

1 Now that you know the ADFGX cipher, you can use your transmitters to send messages with Morse code. Ready, set, go!

2 Check the chart on the left for the signals for A, D, F, G, and X.

3 Practice these five letters in Morse code until you feel like an expert, and review your sender's and receiver's signals on page 11.

4 It's time to send messages! Station your friend in a secret spot, find a hiding place for yourself (not more than 100 yards [100 meters] away from your friend), and Morse away! Test your friend to see if he really understands your message by sending him your hiding place

using the ADFGX cipher. See if he can find you. And if you're receiving a message, don't forget to write down the letters so that you can decipher them, or else your message will be lost in radio space!

MORE FROM HEADQUARTERS

1 One letter was left out of the ADFGX grid. Did you notice which one it was? What would you do if one of the words of your message included that letter? Think of some solutions, then see what real spies do in **What's the Secret?** on the next page.

2 Look at the number/letter grid below. It can be used the same way you used the ADFGX grid to encipher messages.

	1	2	3	4	5	6
1	A	B	C	D	E	F
2	G	H	I	J	K	L
3	M	N	O	P	Q	R
4	S	T	U	V	W	X
5	Y	Z				

This time, the letters from a message are enciphered by substituting a pair of *numbers*, giving the number from the far left column first, then the number from the top row. For example, the letter K would be enciphered 25. A dot is placed between each letter, and a space is left between each word. SECRET CODE would be enciphered as: **41.15.13.36.15.42   13.33.14.15**.

3 Can you decipher the following message? (You can check your answer on page 48.)

**51.33.43.36   32.15.46.42   31.23.41.41.23.33.32
23.41   23.32   22.33.26.26.51.45.33.33.14**

4 Rearrange the letters in the number/letter grid to create your own cipher. For example, you could arrange the letters of the alphabet in columns instead of in rows. Can you think of other ways to arrange the alphabet in the grid?

WHAT'S THE SECRET?

Since some letters appear more frequently than others in words, the ADFGX cipher would have been pretty easy to decipher if the same cipher was used for several weeks at a time. However, the Germans would change the letter location in the grid every day, making it more difficult to decipher intercepted messages.

One problem with a five-by-five grid is that it only has space for twenty-five letters, so one letter is always left out. In our version, the letter Y is left out. When Y appears in a message, it's sometimes replaced with the letter I so that XD stands for both I and Y. It's up to the person receiving the cipher to figure out which letter to use.

(continued from page 9)

"**B**ut Ms. Lightly," you say, instead of erasing the letters. "Who do you think wrote this?"

"Who do *you* think wrote it?" she asks.

Ms. Lightly was always doing that kind of thing—turning your questions around and making *you* answer them!

"Maybe some kids were playing around in here after school on Friday?" you suggest.

"That sounds like a reasonable guess," she says. "It looks like a bunch of nonsense to me."

And with that, she reaches for the eraser and wipes the letters off the board.

"Now let's get that math problem up there so we can talk about it," she says.

■ Too bad! You didn't get anywhere by questioning Ms. Lightly. Go back and try again!

On March 5, 1918, French radio operators intercepted the first German messages that used the ADFGX cipher. For the rest of that month, the French continued to collect ADFGX messages, but since the Germans were changing the cipher every day (by rearranging the grid), French cryptologists were stumped.

But not for long. On April 1, 1918, enough intercepted messages came in that French cryptologist Captain Georges Painvin made a breakthrough. He found that the opening sections of two intercepted messages were similar, and he soon realized that the cipher was based on a five-letter checkerboard concept. With this information, he was able to figure out the cipher for that one day.

After that break, the French discovered that the Germans had added a sixth letter, V, to the ADFGX combination, so that numerals could also be enciphered (previously, numbers had to be spelled out). Still, Painvin was able to break this code, again for the single day that cipher was used—June 2, 1918.

Using information from deciphered ADFGX messages, the Allies were able to get their armies ready to fight off a German attack on June 9, 1918. That battle was a turning point in the war, beginning a series of victories for the Allies.

The true story of how Painvin broke the ADFGX cipher was not revealed until many years after the war was over.

OPERATION
crack
THE SCRAMBLE

#8

By now, you know a lot of complex **codes** and **ciphers** that can be used to send secret messages. But sometimes a spy has to act fast and **encode** something on the spot. That's when scrambled words come in handy. They might be easier to figure out than other codes you've learned, but at least the average person can't read them at a glance. So take a crack at these scrambled words. See which ones appeal to you!

STUFF YOU'LL NEED
● **Pencil and paper**

WHAT YOU DO

PART 1:
STRATEGY TIME!

Figuring out scrambled word codes takes practice. The more scrambled codes you **decode**, the better you'll get at it. Here are a few tips that'll help you figure out these and other codes.

1 Try to decode the two- and three-letter words in any sentence first. Look for the common ones like: *if, of, so, to, be, on, no, and, the,* and so on. If you can figure out the smaller words, you might be able to find the **message key** for the entire message.

2 Try reading the message in lots of different ways (like backward or in the mirror). Give yourself some time to think. When you try decoding the scrambled messages in Part 2, don't peek at the answers until you've figured out the message keys. We've turned the answers upside down to help keep them out of sight, but you should still cover up each answer with a piece of paper.

PART 2:
CRACK THE SCRAMBLES

1. Mix it up!
Try to decode this message:

CAHE RWDO SAH TSI TTEERLS XIMDE PU

Answer (turn over):

Did you figure out the code already? Good work! The message key is to mix up the letters in each word. The message reads: "Each word has its letters mixed up."

2. The Old Switcheroo
Try to decode this message:

THIM SESSAGI EE SAST YD
OECODI EY FOK UNOH WOW

Answer (turn over):

Do you know the coding rule for this sentence? The message key is to exchange the last letter in each word with the first letter in the next. The message reads: "This message is easy to decode if you know how."

29

3. Something's Missing

Try to decode this message:

**LTHGH THS MSSG SMS STRNG,
T SHLD B SY T RD**

Answer (turn over):

Can you figure out the coding rule? The message key is to remove all the vowels from the words. The message reads: "Although this message seems strange, it should be easy to read."

4. Mirror, Mirror

Try to decode this message:

YAW SIHT ETIRW YEHT SEIRTNUOC EMOS NI

Answer (turn over):

Can you figure out the coding rule? Did holding the message in front of a mirror help? The message key here is to write the sentence backward, from left to right. The message reads: "In some countries they write this way."

MORE FROM HEADQUARTERS

1 Can you figure out the messages below? Each uses one of the coding methods you practiced in this activity. Check page 48 for the answers.

    a. THL EAUNCW HILB LA ED TAWN
    b. TNEGA ELBUOD FO ERAWEB
    c. OUY RAE GBINE LLOOWEFD
    d. SCRT MTNG T MDNGHT

2 Try to decode this secret message. It combines two of the coding methods you learned in this activity. When you combine two codes it's called **double encrypting**. Again, you'll find the answer on page 48.

**NOITSEUE QHS TT IAHE TDOO
CT TOR NE ODOO CT**

---

3 Write a message to a friend using one of the methods above. Don't give her the message key. Can she decode the message?

4 Visit the Spy University web site at **www.scholastic.com/spy** to decode more scrambled messages!

(continued from page 12 or 32)

You get to school early the next day—even earlier than yesterday. You head right for your classroom. But this time, when you arrive at the door, there's a note taped to it. You quickly look both ways to make sure no one's around, and then you carefully peel the note off the door. You open the folded paper and read it. It says: **thgilrats worromot**.

thgilrats worromot

At first glance, it looks like the note's about rats and worms—but no, of course, it's another code! You look at your watch, and you wonder if you have time to copy the message down before Ms. Lightly arrives. But then, as you look at the handwriting, you suddenly get the feeling that you've seen it somewhere before. Maybe you should keep the note, so you can figure out why the handwriting looks so familiar....

- If you decide to keep the note, turn to **page 37**.
- If you decide to copy the note and put it back as fast as you can, turn to **page 41**.

9

OPERATION
codebuster

So, you want to be a **code** buster? You'll be off to the right start if you're good at crossword puzzles or word games like hangman (see **What's the Secret?** on page 33 for more info on this). This activity will give you a good set of code-busting strategies, so read on and catch a code!

STUFF YOU'LL NEED

- **Pencil and paper**
- **Cipher wheel (see page 16)—optional**

WHAT YOU DO

1 Suppose you intercepted the following message:

**MAX YTNEM EBXL GHM BG HNK LMTKL
UNM BG HNKLXEOXL — LATDXLIXTKX**

How would you begin to **decipher** it?

2 You could start by learning the letters that are used most often in the English language. Check out this list. The letters are in order from *most* frequently used to *least* frequently used:

E T A O N I R S H D L U C M P F Y W G B V J K X Q Z

Knowing that E is the most popular letter in the English language will help you a lot in your deciphering!

3 To begin deciphering the message, make an alphabet chart and fill in the number of times each letter appears in the **enciphered** message. Place a check next to the letter each time you see it.

4 Now look at your chart. Count the number of checks for each letter, and write that number beside the checks. Then circle the most commonly used letters, and place a star beside the letters that are used the very most.

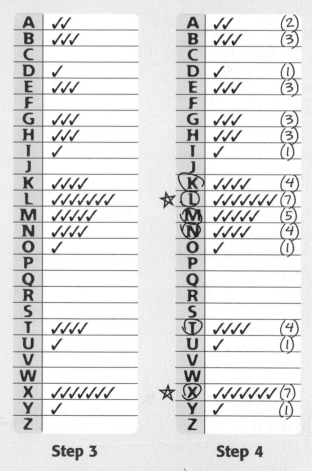

Step 3

Step 4

5 The most commonly used letters in the enciphered message are L, X, M, N, K, and T. Since E is the most commonly used letter in English,

one of those letters is probably E. You just have to find out which one! So, to start, align the letter L on the inner disk of your cipher wheel with the letter E on the outer wheel. (Or, if you're doing this the hard way, write out a Caesar cipher in strip form, shifting the lower alphabet so that L is below E.) Try to decipher the message using that shift. Does it work?

6 If that shift doesn't work, try lining up the X underneath the E on your cipher wheel. If that

doesn't break the cipher, then try M, N, K, and T. Not every message will have E as the *most* common letter, but it should be *one* of the commonly used letters. Just keep trying options until you're able to decipher the message. Here's a hint: It's a famous quote from Shakespeare's *Julius Caesar* (since you're working with the Caesar cipher after all!). You can check your answer on page 48.

MORE FROM HEADQUARTERS

1 Have your friend write a simple message using a Caesar cipher strip or the cipher wheel. The message should be about ten to fifteen words long. When you receive the message, try to break the cipher by figuring out the most commonly used letters.

2 The game of hangman helps sharpen your code-breaking skills. In case you've never played it before, here are the instructions: Have a friend think of a word and then draw a short line for every letter in that word. Begin the game by asking your friend if a certain letter is in the word. If it is, your friend should write that letter on the appropriate line. If it isn't, your friend gets to draw a part of a body to be hanged,

beginning with a head, followed by the body, arms, and legs. Use your knowledge of the most commonly used letters to help make your letter choices (start with E!). After you've chosen several correct letters, try to guess the word your friend picked. If your friend finishes drawing the hangman before you guess

SPYquest

(*continued from page 9*)

You quickly write the letters down in your notebook. After you and Ms. Lightly discuss the math problem, you return to your desk and start decoding.

You can see that one letter is used most often, and that there are a few easy two-letter words. With these clues, you're able to decipher the message in a snap using the techniques you learned in **Operation Code Buster**.

Even though you're happy that you decoded the message, you also find it very worrying. What's going on with Ms. Lightly? What does she have to hide?

- If you decide to follow Ms. Lightly after school, turn to **page 12**.

- If you decide to come to school early again tomorrow to get more clues, turn to **page 30**.

- If you decide to wait until Wednesday afternoon, turn to **page 18**.

PHHW PH RQ
ZHGQHVGDB
DW WKUHH

Psst. You can check your answer on page 48!

the word, you lose! For advanced hangman, use phrases instead of words.

3 How fast of a code buster are you? Test your skills on the Spy University web site at **www.scholastic.com/spy!**

WHAT'S THE SECRET?

Long messages are usually easier to break than short ones. The more letters or symbols you have to analyze, the greater the chance that certain letters will be repeated. Check out the code-busting tips on the right for more strategies.

MORE CODE-BUSTING TIPS

▼ **Look for one-letter words.** They're easy! How many one-letter words are there in the English language?

▼ **Look for two-letter words.** Since there are only a few of them in the English language, two-letter words are a good place to start. The most common two-letter words are *of, to, in, is, it, be, by, he, as, on, at, or, an, so, if,* and *no.*

▼ **Look for two of the same letter in a row.** Since you know that certain letters are often doubled in English (like L, E, S, O, and T), you can use double letters to your advantage. Also, since certain letters are never or rarely used twice in a row in English words, you can eliminate some possibilities. For example, you don't see the letters J or W twice in a row in English. Which other letters are never or rarely doubled?

▼ **Look at the beginning and the end of a message for the usual opening and closing phrases** (like "dear" at the beginning or "sincerely" at the end). When you know these phrases, you can use them as a key to break the rest of the code. This trick was widely used during World War II when decoding official messages written by the Japanese, since they always began and ended with the same formalities.

In May 1942, during World War II, the Japanese were preparing a major attack on the United States military in the Central Pacific. The Japanese navy had battleships, cruisers, destroyers, aircraft carriers, and submarines that greatly outnumbered the opposing U.S. fleet. Still, the U.S. wasn't willing to surrender.

The Americans had broken the Japanese naval code and knew that a major attack was coming, but they did not know exactly *where*. Japanese communication named the target by the letters AF. There were many targets in the Central Pacific that could be attacked, such as the Marshall Islands, the Midway Islands, or Oahu in the Hawaiian Islands. No one was sure.

Three naval officers, Joseph Rochefort, E. T. Layton, and W. J. Holmes, solved the mystery with a brilliant plan. The Americans at the Midway base radioed naval headquarters at Pearl Harbor to report that the fresh-water distillation plant at Midway had broken down. The message was deliberately sent using a simple code that they knew the Japanese could break.

Two days later, the Americans intercepted a coded Japanese message. The message reported that AF was short of drinking water because of a plant breakdown. Then, the Americans knew that AF was Midway. So, when the Japanese fleet came charging into the Midway Islands for their major attack, the American fleet was ready and waiting.

The Japanese were taken by surprise and lost four aircraft carriers, 261 aircraft, and one cruiser in the battle that followed.

It was the Japanese navy's first major defeat since 1592, and it ended their control over the Pacific. Most historians agree that the Battle of Midway was the turning point of World War II in the Pacific.

OPERATION CIPHER TABLE

#10

In **Operation Cipher Wheel**, you **enciphered** a message by replacing its letters with a new set of letters that was created by shifting the alphabet a few steps over. But as you saw in **Operation Code Buster**, those simple **ciphers** are easy to break by looking at which letters appear most often in the cipher and matching those up with the most frequently used letters in English.

So, what can you do to make sure your ciphers remain unbroken? Try this activity to learn a more complex cipher that's built around a special **key word**. It was invented by Blaise de Vigenere (pronounced VIG-IN-EER) in the sixteenth century, so it's often called the Vigenere cipher. For hundreds of years after its invention, it was considered nearly impossible to **decipher**, because frequently used letters couldn't be used as clues.

WHAT YOU DO

1 You've intercepted the following secret message.

BHBIGV XFMALH ANEIQS QNJMVG BIK

Can you decipher it using the techniques you learned in **Operation Code Buster**?

2 No luck? Now you know why this cipher was considered indecipherable for so many years! In this system, the same shifted alphabet is not used for each letter. Instead, six different shifted alphabets are used! A key word determines which alphabet will be used for each letter. For this message, the key word is TUXEDO.

Cipher table

A	B	C	D	E	F	G	H	I	J	K	L	M	N	O	P	Q	R	S	T	U	V	W	X	Y	Z
B	C	D	E	F	G	H	I	J	K	L	M	N	O	P	Q	R	S	T	U	V	W	X	Y	Z	A
C	D	E	F	G	H	I	J	K	L	M	N	O	P	Q	R	S	T	U	V	W	X	Y	Z	A	B
D	E	F	G	H	I	J	K	L	M	N	O	P	Q	R	S	T	U	V	W	X	Y	Z	A	B	C
E	F	G	H	I	J	K	L	M	N	O	P	Q	R	S	T	U	V	W	X	Y	Z	A	B	C	D
F	G	H	I	J	K	L	M	N	O	P	Q	R	S	T	U	V	W	X	Y	Z	A	B	C	D	E
G	H	I	J	K	L	M	N	O	P	Q	R	S	T	U	V	W	X	Y	Z	A	B	C	D	E	F
H	I	J	K	L	M	N	O	P	Q	R	S	T	U	V	W	X	Y	Z	A	B	C	D	E	F	G
I	J	K	L	M	N	O	P	Q	R	S	T	U	V	W	X	Y	Z	A	B	C	D	E	F	G	H
J	K	L	M	N	O	P	Q	R	S	T	U	V	W	X	Y	Z	A	B	C	D	E	F	G	H	I
K	L	M	N	O	P	Q	R	S	T	U	V	W	X	Y	Z	A	B	C	D	E	F	G	H	I	J
L	M	N	O	P	Q	R	S	T	U	V	W	X	Y	Z	A	B	C	D	E	F	G	H	I	J	K
M	N	O	P	Q	R	S	T	U	V	W	X	Y	Z	A	B	C	D	E	F	G	H	I	J	K	L
N	O	P	Q	R	S	T	U	V	W	X	Y	Z	A	B	C	D	E	F	G	H	I	J	K	L	M
O	P	Q	R	S	T	U	V	W	X	Y	Z	A	B	C	D	E	F	G	H	I	J	K	L	M	N
P	Q	R	S	T	U	V	W	X	Y	Z	A	B	C	D	E	F	G	H	I	J	K	L	M	N	O
Q	R	S	T	U	V	W	X	Y	Z	A	B	C	D	E	F	G	H	I	J	K	L	M	N	O	P
R	S	T	U	V	W	X	Y	Z	A	B	C	D	E	F	G	H	I	J	K	L	M	N	O	P	Q
S	T	U	V	W	X	Y	Z	A	B	C	D	E	F	G	H	I	J	K	L	M	N	O	P	Q	R
T	U	V	W	X	Y	Z	A	B	C	D	E	F	G	H	I	J	K	L	M	N	O	P	Q	R	S
U	V	W	X	Y	Z	A	B	C	D	E	F	G	H	I	J	K	L	M	N	O	P	Q	R	S	T
V	W	X	Y	Z	A	B	C	D	E	F	G	H	I	J	K	L	M	N	O	P	Q	R	S	T	U
W	X	Y	Z	A	B	C	D	E	F	G	H	I	J	K	L	M	N	O	P	Q	R	S	T	U	V
X	Y	Z	A	B	C	D	E	F	G	H	I	J	K	L	M	N	O	P	Q	R	S	T	U	V	W
Y	Z	A	B	C	D	E	F	G	H	I	J	K	L	M	N	O	P	Q	R	S	T	U	V	W	X
Z	A	B	C	D	E	F	G	H	I	J	K	L	M	N	O	P	Q	R	S	T	U	V	W	X	Y

34

3 To learn how this cipher works, have a look at the **cipher tables** on these pages. A cipher table is created by writing out the alphabet in twenty-six rows, starting with the normal alphabet on top, then shifting the alphabet one letter to the right in each of the next rows. So, the first row starts with A, the next with B, the next with C, and so on.

4 To encipher the phrase "What a great cipher" using the cipher table and the key word TUXEDO, you start by writing the message. Then, above it, write the key word as many times as necessary for the length of the message. Keep the letters of the key word lined up with the letters of the message.

A	B	C	D	E	F	G	H	I	J	K	L	M	N	O	P	Q	R	S	T	U	V	W	X	Y	Z
B	C	D	E	F	G	H	I	J	K	L	M	N	O	P	Q	R	S	T	U	V	W	X	Y	Z	A
C	D	E	F	G	H	I	J	K	L	M	N	O	P	Q	R	S	T	U	V	W	X	Y	Z	A	B
D	E	F	G	H	I	J	K	L	M	N	O	P	Q	R	S	T	U	V	W	X	Y	Z	A	B	C
E	F	G	H	I	J	K	L	M	N	O	P	Q	R	S	T	U	V	W	X	Y	Z	A	B	C	D
F	G	H	I	J	K	L	M	N	O	P	Q	R	S	T	U	V	W	X	Y	Z	A	B	C	D	E
G	H	I	J	K	L	M	N	O	P	Q	R	S	T	U	V	W	X	Y	Z	A	B	C	D	E	F
H	I	J	K	L	M	N	O	P	Q	R	S	T	U	V	W	X	Y	Z	A	B	C	D	E	F	G
I	J	K	L	M	N	O	P	Q	R	S	T	U	V	W	X	Y	Z	A	B	C	D	E	F	G	H
J	K	L	M	N	O	P	Q	R	S	T	U	V	W	X	Y	Z	A	B	C	D	E	F	G	H	I
K	L	M	N	O	P	Q	R	S	T	U	V	W	X	Y	Z	A	B	C	D	E	F	G	H	I	J
L	M	N	O	P	Q	R	S	T	U	V	W	X	Y	Z	A	B	C	D	E	F	G	H	I	J	K
M	N	O	P	Q	R	S	T	U	V	W	X	Y	Z	A	B	C	D	E	F	G	H	I	J	K	L
N	O	P	Q	R	S	T	U	V	W	X	Y	Z	A	B	C	D	E	F	G	H	I	J	K	L	M
O	P	Q	R	S	T	U	V	W	X	Y	Z	A	B	C	D	E	F	G	H	I	J	K	L	M	N
P	Q	R	S	T	U	V	W	X	Y	Z	A	B	C	D	E	F	G	H	I	J	K	L	M	N	O
Q	R	S	T	U	V	W	X	Y	Z	A	B	C	D	E	F	G	H	I	J	K	L	M	N	O	P
R	S	T	U	V	W	X	Y	Z	A	B	C	D	E	F	G	H	I	J	K	L	M	N	O	P	Q
S	T	U	V	W	X	Y	Z	A	B	C	D	E	F	G	H	I	J	K	L	M	N	O	P	Q	R
T	U	V	W	X	Y	Z	A	B	C	D	E	F	G	H	I	J	K	L	M	N	O	P	Q	R	S
U	V	W	X	Y	Z	A	B	C	D	E	F	G	H	I	J	K	L	M	N	O	P	Q	R	S	T
V	W	X	Y	Z	A	B	C	D	E	F	G	H	I	J	K	L	M	N	O	P	Q	R	S	T	U
W	X	Y	Z	A	B	C	D	E	F	G	H	I	J	K	L	M	N	O	P	Q	R	S	T	U	V
X	Y	Z	A	B	C	D	E	F	G	H	I	J	K	L	M	N	O	P	Q	R	S	T	U	V	W
Y	Z	A	B	C	D	E	F	G	H	I	J	K	L	M	N	O	P	Q	R	S	T	U	V	W	X
Z	A	B	C	D	E	F	G	H	I	J	K	L	M	N	O	P	Q	R	S	T	U	V	W	X	Y

T	U	X	E	D	O	T	U	X	E	D	O	T	U	X	E
W	H	A	T	A	G	R	E	A	T	C	I	P	H	E	R

5 The key word letter tells you which row of the cipher table to use to encipher that letter. For example, W is enciphered with the row that begins with the letter T. In the cipher table on this page, look across the row that begins with the letter T until you come to the column that lines up with the letter W in the top row, and you get the letter P. That's the first letter in the enciphered message.

Key word>	T	U	X	E	D	O	T	U	X	E	D	O	T	U	X	E
Message>	W	H	A	T	A	G	R	E	A	T	C	I	P	H	E	R
Enciphered message>	P															

6 Repeat step 5 for each letter of the message.

Key word>	T	U	X	E	D	O	T	U	X	E	D	O	T	U	X	E
Message>	W	H	A	T	A	G	R	E	A	T	C	I	P	H	E	R
Enciphered message>	P	B	X	X	D	U	K	Y	X	X	F	W	I	B	B	V

7 To make your message even *harder* to decipher, divide the letters into TUXEDO groups,

so the groups are all six letters long, except for the last one, which can be however long it needs to be to finish the message. When the message looks like this, the code buster won't be able to figure out the easy little words (like the one-, two-, and three-letter words). This means, though, that the receiver of the message will have to separate the deciphered letters back into their original words (which shouldn't be too hard).

Step 5

Key word>	T	U	X	E	D	O		T	U	X	E	D	O		T	U	X	E
Message>	W	H	A	T	A	G		R	E	A	T	C	I		P	H	E	R
Enciphered message>	P	B	X	X	D	U		K	Y	X	X	F	W		I	B	B	V

8 To **decipher** a message that uses a cipher table system, follow these steps. First, write the key word letters above the enciphered message. Let's use the message from step 1.

T	U	X	E	D	O		T	U	X	E	D	O		T	U	X	E	D	O		T	U	X	E	D	O		T	U	X
B	H	B	I	G	V		X	F	M	A	L	H		A	N	E	I	Q	S		Q	N	J	M	V	G		B	I	K

35

A	B	C	D	E	F	G	H	I	J	K	L	M	N	O	P	Q	R	S	T	U	V	W	X	Y	Z
B	C	D	E	F	G	H	I	J	K	L	M	N	O	P	Q	R	S	T	U	V	W	X	Y	Z	A
C	D	E	F	G	H	I	J	K	L	M	N	O	P	Q	R	S	T	U	V	W	X	Y	Z	A	B
D	E	F	G	H	I	J	K	L	M	N	O	P	Q	R	S	T	U	V	W	X	Y	Z	A	B	C
E	F	G	H	I	J	K	L	M	N	O	P	Q	R	S	T	U	V	W	X	Y	Z	A	B	C	D
F	G	H	I	J	K	L	M	N	O	P	Q	R	S	T	U	V	W	X	Y	Z	A	B	C	D	E
G	H	I	J	K	L	M	N	O	P	Q	R	S	T	U	V	W	X	Y	Z	A	B	C	D	E	F
H	I	J	K	L	M	N	O	P	Q	R	S	T	U	V	W	X	Y	Z	A	B	C	D	E	F	G
I	J	K	L	M	N	O	P	Q	R	S	T	U	V	W	X	Y	Z	A	B	C	D	E	F	G	H
J	K	L	M	N	O	P	Q	R	S	T	U	V	W	X	Y	Z	A	B	C	D	E	F	G	H	I
K	L	M	N	O	P	Q	R	S	T	U	V	W	X	Y	Z	A	B	C	D	E	F	G	H	I	J
L	M	N	O	P	Q	R	S	T	U	V	W	X	Y	Z	A	B	C	D	E	F	G	H	I	J	K
M	N	O	P	Q	R	S	T	U	V	W	X	Y	Z	A	B	C	D	E	F	G	H	I	J	K	L
N	O	P	Q	R	S	T	U	V	W	X	Y	Z	A	B	C	D	E	F	G	H	I	J	K	L	M
O	P	Q	R	S	T	U	V	W	X	Y	Z	A	B	C	D	E	F	G	H	I	J	K	L	M	N
P	Q	R	S	T	U	V	W	X	Y	Z	A	B	C	D	E	F	G	H	I	J	K	L	M	N	O
Q	R	S	T	U	V	W	X	Y	Z	A	B	C	D	E	F	G	H	I	J	K	L	M	N	O	P
R	S	T	U	V	W	X	Y	Z	A	B	C	D	E	F	G	H	I	J	K	L	M	N	O	P	Q
S	T	U	V	W	X	Y	Z	A	B	C	D	E	F	G	H	I	J	K	L	M	N	O	P	Q	R
T	U	V	W	X	Y	Z	A	B	C	D	E	F	G	H	I	J	K	L	M	N	O	P	Q	R	S
U	V	W	X	Y	Z	A	B	C	D	E	F	G	H	I	J	K	L	M	N	O	P	Q	R	S	T
V	W	X	Y	Z	A	B	C	D	E	F	G	H	I	J	K	L	M	N	O	P	Q	R	S	T	U
W	X	Y	Z	A	B	C	D	E	F	G	H	I	J	K	L	M	N	O	P	Q	R	S	T	U	V
X	Y	Z	A	B	C	D	E	F	G	H	I	J	K	L	M	N	O	P	Q	R	S	T	U	V	W
Y	Z	A	B	C	D	E	F	G	H	I	J	K	L	M	N	O	P	Q	R	S	T	U	V	W	X
Z	A	B	C	D	E	F	G	H	I	J	K	L	M	N	O	P	Q	R	S	T	U	V	W	X	Y

Step 9

9 For each letter, use the alphabet row indicated by the letter in the key word. So, for the first letter, look at the T row, and find the letter B. Look all the way up the column to the top row, and you'll find the original letter (I). Finish deciphering the message from step 1. Can you do it now? To check your answer, look on page 48.

T	U	X	E	D	O		T	U	X	E	D	O		T	U	X	E	D	O		T	U	X	E	D	O		T	U	X
B	H	B	I	G	V		X	F	M	A	L	H		A	N	E	I	Q	S		Q	N	J	M	V	G		B	I	K
I																														

MORE FROM HEADQUARTERS

1 Make up your own key word. It should not have any letters repeated, and it should be about five or six letters long. Then use that key word to encipher a message!

2 On the Spy University web site at **www.scholastic.com/spy**, you can

use a cipher machine to make and break these kinds of ciphers in the click of a mouse!

WHAT'S THE SECRET?

When it comes time to decipher intercepted messages, there are certain patterns in the words and letters that code busters look for. You learned some of these strategies in **Operation Code Buster**, like checking for frequently used letters, figuring out the little words first, looking for letters repeated right next to each other, and so on. Those are clues that can break a code wide open.

However, by using a different alphabet to encipher each letter, you're making sure that these clues won't be available, so the enciphered message will be more difficult to break. It takes more time to encipher messages with the cipher table system, but it's worth it!

Even the sculptures at the CIA (Central Intelligence Agency) headquarters in McLean, Virginia, hold secret messages. In a courtyard on the closely guarded campus, there is a copper sculpture called "Kryptos" that was designed by an architect named Jim Sanborn. Kryptos stands more than six feet high and looks like a scroll. On the scroll are letters that seem to make no sense. However, on the right side of the sculpture is a cipher table with carved letters that can be used to decipher part of the 865-letter message.

The entire message on the scroll has never been fully deciphered, but many code breakers continue to try. So far, they've figured out all but the final ninety-seven letters! The complete solution is known only to the sculptor and the CIA director, who keeps the secret locked in a safe (to be passed on to each new director).

(continued from page 30)

You decide to keep the note, but instead of putting it away immediately, you study it for a few moments. You realize that the two words are just written backward, nothing too complicated. Starlight tomorrow. What does that mean? You wonder about this for a while, and then you focus on the handwriting, trying to figure out where you've seen it before.

Just then, you realize something important—what if Ms. Lightly is expecting this note? What will she think when it's not there? And what will happen if she doesn't get the information in the message? You quickly tape the note back to the door.

But just as you're doing this, Ms. Lightly turns the corner. She sees what you've done and raises her eyebrows.

"What's this?" she asks, taking the note from the door and unfolding it. As soon as she sees what's inside, she looks annoyed.

"Did you think this note was for you?" she asks.

You shake your head.

"I was just curious," you say.

"You wouldn't like it if *I* read *your* notes," she says. "Would you?"

You shake your head again.

"This is just a bunch of nonsense anyway," she says. "It's nothing important."

And with that, she enters the class-room, folding the note and putting it inside her pocket.

On Wednesday afternoon, nothing happens that's out of the ordinary. You wait for something to happen at three, but Ms. Lightly just stays in her room, helping students with their math until four.

For the rest of the year, you never see another message, and Ms. Lightly never mentions them again. You decide to believe that they were nothing important, but still, you're stuck with a nagging feeling that you should have known where you'd seen that hand-writing before….

■ Oh, well—the quest didn't work out this way. Go back and try again!

The Kryptos sculpture at CIA headquarters.

OPERATION SPYcode

#11

Here's another **cipher** that uses a **key word**, like the cipher you learned in the previous operation. This time, though, the key word is used to set up a special cipher grid that scrambles up the alphabet. With the alphabet out of order, code busters will get all mixed-up, too!

STUFF YOU'LL NEED

- **Pencil and paper**
- **Cipher wheel (see page 16)—optional**

YOUR NETWORK

- **A friend to receive your messages**

WHAT YOU DO

PART 1: THE KEY WORD

1 Try to **decipher** the following message. You can use your **cipher wheel** and what you learned about deciphering messages in **Operation Code Buster** to help you.

ZVP AYHU YQ NDZ NB ZVP KSLP

This is a tough one, but don't give up. Read on!

2 This cipher uses a key word to set up a grid of letters. In this case, the key word is really two

(continued from page 15)

It's a little after 3:00, and you arrive, completely out of breath, at the Starlight Cinema. It's totally deserted, since the next movie isn't until 5:30. You wait for fifteen minutes, but it becomes clear that nothing's going to happen here. Too bad you can't get to the café in time!

■ This was a dead end! Go back and try again.

words: SPY CODE. To begin, write the key word on the top line of the grid. Then write the rest of the letters of the alphabet in order underneath the key word, but skip all the letters that appear in the key word (in this case, the letters **S**, **P**, **Y**, **C**, **O**, **D**, and **E**).

S	P	Y	C	O	D	E
A	B	F	G	H	I	J
K	L	M	N	Q	R	T
U	V	W	X	Z		

3 Next, place the letters under an alphabet in the vertical order in which they appear: **S**, **A**, **K**, **U**, **P**, **B**, and so on. Can you figure out the message now? Use the same method you used for Caesar ciphers. Find each letter from the enciphered message in the lower alphabet and look directly above it for the real letter. Turn to page 48 to check your answer.

A	B	C	D	E	F	G	H	I	J	K	L	M	N	O	P	Q	R	S	T	U	V	W	X	Y	Z
S	A	K	U	P	B	L	V	Y	F	M	W	C	G	N	X	O	H	Q	Z	D	I	R	E	J	T

PART 2: THE KEY NUMBER

1 A variation of this cipher uses the key word in another way. Suppose that SPY CODE is still the key word. First, arrange the letters in the key word in alphabetical order. In this case the order is: **C, D, E, O, P, S, Y.**

2 Next, each letter is given a number based on its alphabetical order (**C=1, D=2, E=3, O=4, P=5, S=6, Y=7**).

3 Now, the key word is written along the top of the cipher grid using the number that corresponds to each letter. The letters of the alphabet are then written below the numbers.

4 Finally, the letters are written below the alphabet in the order that they appear in each vertical column, beginning with the column with 1 on top, followed by the column with 2 on top, and so on.

6	5	7	1	4	2	3
A	B	C	D	E	F	G
H	I	J	K	L	M	N
O	P	Q	R	S	T	U
V	W	X	Y	Z		

A	B	C	D	E	F	G	H	I	J	K	L	M	N	O	P	Q	R	S	T	U	V	W	X	Y	Z
D	K	R	Y	F	M	T	G	N	U	E	L	S	Z	B	I	P	W	A	H	O	V	C	J	Q	X

5 Now you can **encipher** a message using this scrambled alphabet system. As usual, find each letter of your message in the top alphabet and encipher it with the letter directly underneath. Try it! Send a message to a friend, making sure he knows the key word and how to work with it in number form.

MORE FROM HEADQUARTERS

1 Use the key word SPY CODE to decipher the following messages:

    a. PEXPKZ IYQYZ ZNGYLVZ
    b. CPPZ CP SZ HPKPQQ
    c. CSZZVPR YQ S QXJ

2 Use the SPY CODE key number system in Part 2 to decipher the following messages:

    a. KFCDWF BM UBWYDZ
    b. SDHG GBSFCBWE NA MOZ
    c. HWBOKLF DGFDY N ZFFY GFLI

3 Make your own key word that will become the top line of your cipher grid. The length of the key word (or words) determines the size of the grid. SPY CODE has seven letters, so the grid is seven spaces across. If you used the word SPYING, your grid would have only six spaces across. The key word or phrase should not have any letters that repeat.

4 Use the key word you chose in #3 to create a key number for a cipher grid. Now your key word can be used for two different ciphers!

WHAT'S THE SECRET?

Using a key word is a great way to complicate your ciphers. In this cipher, the key word creates a scrambled alphabet that's very difficult to figure out without the **message key**.

If you want to throw off enemy code breakers even more, create a set of key words and a schedule for using them. You could use a different key word (or key number) system for each day of the week!

One of the most famous secret-message stories in history involved Mary, Queen of Scots. In 1558, Elizabeth I, a Protestant, was crowned the queen of England. Mary, a Catholic, was seen by some as the rightful queen and therefore was considered a threat to Elizabeth's rule. After Mary was found to be involved in a conspiracy against Elizabeth and her government, she was imprisoned in the Tower of London. While there, Mary wrote coded messages that were smuggled out by Gilbert Gifford, a man she thought she could trust. But Gifford was actually a spy for Elizabeth! When Elizabeth was told of the messages, she had Mary beheaded for treason. You can never be too careful, aspiring spies!

OPERATION
bookworm
CODE

#12

Y ou learned how to hide a message in a message in **Operation Deeper Meaning**. How about hiding a message in a book? No problem! Just find the right book, and your message is already there. How's that possible? Read on!

WHAT YOU DO

PART 1: DECODE!

1 Look at the **coded** message below.

> 12.5.7
> 13.13.6
> 12.8.4
> 12.2.8
> 13.10.6

2 The message is broken down into sets of three numbers. The first number stands for the page number, and the second stands for a line number on that page (starting at the top of the page and not counting headings). The third number stands for the number of words you should move along the selected line.

3 Use the code in step 1 to find the secret message on the pages at right. Remember, don't count the heading ("The Journey Home") as a line! Check your answer on page 48.

PART 2: ENCODE!

1 Use one of your own books to send a message to a friend. Either choose a book that your friend also has (like your math textbook), or plan to give the book to your friend after you're done encoding. The easiest and safest option is to use a book that your friend has, too.

12

THE JOURNEY HOME

❧

I t had been a long time since Jack had seen his home. For years he'd been at sea, traveling the world. He'd thought that he would never come home again. But when he received the telephone call telling him that his sister was getting married, he knew he had to return home. So, on a Friday morning, Jack took the long walk up the street to the house that

2 Look through the book for the words you need. As you find them, note the page number, line number, and word number on a piece of paper. For the line number, don't count chapter titles or any other headings.

3 Now you're ready to send your code. Make sure your friend knows the system and has the right book. If you have to hand over your own copy of the book, think of a clever way to do this. If you use a library book, you might even tell your friend where to find it on the shelves (using the call number). Whatever you do, it's best to pass the book and the code at different times.

WHAT'S THE SECRET?

As long as you keep the coded message and the book separate, no one will have any idea what all those numbers are supposed to mean.

13

he'd called home for so long. As he opened the gate to his front yard, he noticed that it still squeaked as it always had. Sitting on the front steps was Rusty, his kid brother, grown up now, but still looking the same as he had seven years before.

Rusty lifted his head and said, "It's good to have you here, Jack."

That's what makes this such a great code. The only problem is finding all the words you need inside the book. That takes a little patience—and a lot of reading—but it's worth it!

MORE FROM HEADQUARTERS

Add a fourth number to the set, and not only will you have a page number, a line number, and a word number, but you'll also have a *letter* number. Then, instead of hunting through the book for the exact words you need, you can just build each word out of letters. For example, in the book shown here, 12.1.2.3 would represent the letter D.

SPYquest

(continued from page 30)

You quickly copy the message into your notebook, fold the message back up, and stick it back on the door. You decide to head outside, so you can decode in private. As you sit down and look at your notebook, you suddenly realize what the message says. You could have decoded it without even copying it down! You just had to come at it from a different direction....

But still, even though you know what the message *says*, you have no idea what it *means*. What does starlight have to do with anything? Does this mean it's going to be a clear night tomorrow?

■ If you decide to do some research to figure out what "starlight" might mean, turn to **page 15**.

■ If you decide to follow Ms. Lightly after school tomorrow, turn to **page 21**.

BREAKING THE ENIGMA CIPHER

During times of war, one side's **code** makers and the other side's code breakers are locked in a constant battle of brain power. The code makers have to assume that their messages will be intercepted, so they try to design codes that'll be impossible for the other side's code breakers to figure out. The more complicated the code, the safer the message. Or so it's hoped.

An "enigma" is a puzzle that's complex and hard to explain or understand.

During World War II, the German military used a **cipher** device that was so complicated, they were sure its ciphers could never be broken. It was called the Enigma machine.

The ciphers the Enigma machine created weren't anything new. They were substitution ciphers in which one letter was replaced by another according to some rule. The ciphers you created with your **cipher wheel** are examples of substitution ciphers. They encipher messages by shifting the alphabet a few steps over (so A becomes D, B becomes E, and so on).

But the ciphers created by your cipher wheel don't take much skill to crack. The code breaker only needs to find out how

This version of the Enigma machine, which has four rotors and some Japanese lettering, was used for secret communication with Germany's ally, Japan.

many letters the alphabet has been shifted (that's the **message key**, or the rules of the code system), and he can figure out the code. Since there are only twenty-five possible ways the alphabet can be shifted (one for each letter after A), the code breaker just has to try each of the twenty-five message keys until one of them works. Easy, right? But that's bad news for someone who wants to send a secret message that won't be **decoded**. That's what's so amazing about the Enigma machine: It creates a cipher that has many more possible message keys—403,291,126,605,635,584,000,000, to be exact!

The basic Enigma was invented in 1918 by Arthur Scherbius in Berlin. Scherbius wanted to create a machine that could use rotors and electrical connections to **encipher** a message. This turned out to be no simple machine!

Here's how it works. The Enigma machine has a keyboard, like a typewriter, but if you type an H on the Enigma, you won't end up with an H! On the Enigma, when a key is pressed (like the H key, for example), an electrical current runs from the key to the plug board, where the letter is changed into another letter (like, for example, R). Then the current passes through a series of four wheels (called rotors) that have the alphabet around them, like the disks of your cipher wheel. At the first rotor, the new letter (R) is changed into another new letter (like V). Then, at the second rotor, the V is changed to a G. The same thing happens at the third and fourth rotors (though early Enigma machines had only three rotors).

After the current passes through the final rotor, a reflector sends the current back through each of the rotors (again changing the letter each time), and finally, an alphabet bulb lights up. This is the first letter of the enciphered message.

The Enigma machine.

KEYBOARD   ROTORS   PLUG BOARD

LIGHTBOARD

43

KEYBOARD   ROTORS   LIGHTBOARD

An overhead view of the Enigma machine.

Whew! Now you can see why they called this machine an *enigma*! But wait—there's more! The next time you press the H key, at least one rotor will shift and the Enigma will put out a different letter. Now *that's* an enigma for sure!

As soon as the Enigma machine was put to use, **cryptologists** began to work on deciphering its messages. Early Enigma ciphers were broken in Poland before WWII, but the Germans kept improving their Enigma machine, so the job of breaking the ciphers got tougher and tougher.

One of the ways the Germans improved the machine was by changing its set-up every day. Each day, the position of the rotors was changed, and the plugs on the plug board were arranged differently. This was called changing the "key setting," and it was done by all Enigma operators on a particular "net" (or network) in the same way and at the same time every day (and later, several times a day). Instructions for each day's key setting were listed in a set of code books kept with each Enigma machine. Every Enigma "net" in the German military had its own set of code

books. These code books were actually more important than the machines themselves, and German military officers were instructed to destroy the code books before the Enigma machines if captured. The Germans knew that if the Allies got their hands on a set of code books, the enciphered messages sent by that particular net would be breakable. So, the race to break the Enigma was never about the machine: It was about the code books.

In 1939, the British intelligence service created a special operation to break the Enigma cipher, known as ULTRA. The first phase of ULTRA was to intercept and collect German radio messages that had been enciphered by the Enigma machine. Next, a group of cryptologists, mathematicians, linguists (people who study languages), and creative thinkers met to examine the messages at a code-breaking facility in Bletchley Park, a short distance outside London. The tools they used included high-

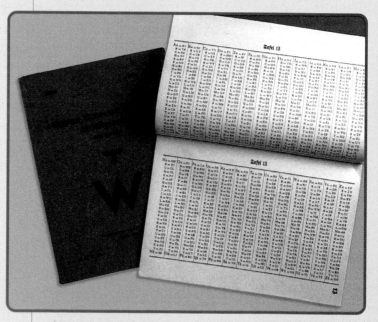

Code books like these were issued to all Enigma operators on German navy vessels. They provided instructions on how to set up the Enigma machine for naval communications each day.

speed calculating machines called "bombes" that were originally invented by Polish cryptologists. The name "bombe" comes from the Polish name for the machine—"bomba"—and not from the kind of *bombs* that explode!

Alan Turing, a brilliant mathematician who worked at Bletchley Park, figured out ways to make the bombe machines more powerful than ever. These machines were called "Turing Bombes," and they could perform mathematical calculations at blazing speeds (at least for that time). Still, though, these machines (together with the cryptologists) couldn't solve the Enigma alone—they needed some clues, and these came from key developments on the war front.

One development that helped the code-breaking efforts greatly was the capture of a set of Enigma code books used by the German navy. This was the result of a mistake made by a German submarine captain named Fritz Julius Lemp on May 9, 1941.

In the middle of a fierce attack on some British ships, Lemp's submarine, the *U-110*, was spotted, and the British ship HMS *Bulldog* was preparing to ram into it. Since Lemp thought his submarine was going to be sunk, he issued the order to abandon ship. He did not destroy his Enigma machine or its code books, since he thought they would go down with the U-110.

But that didn't happen. The British decided to *capture* the submarine, not sink it. Lemp must have realized this as he was swimming away, because he was last seen trying to swim back. Lemp never made it back, though (and must have drowned in the process), so the British were able to board the empty submarine and get both the Enigma machine and the set of code books.

The day after the submarine was captured, the Allies realized that if the Germans knew that the code books had been captured, all of the codes would be changed. To prevent this, the British "accidentally" sunk the submarine as they were towing it back to land so that the Germans would think all of their secrets were safe at the bottom of the ocean.

The mistake made by Captain Lemp wasn't the only one that helped the code breakers along. German cipher clerks also made mistakes—they didn't change the key settings on their machines exactly when they were supposed to, and they sometimes took shortcuts in their procedures. Errors like these gave the code breakers the edge they needed to close in on the Enigma.

An American search party preparing to board a sinking German submarine (called a U-boat—short for "undersea boat").

So, after years of hard work and a little bit of luck, by 1943 the Enigma used by the German navy was no longer an enigma. This meant that intercepted German messages could be deciphered, giving the Allies crucial information about German naval activity. For example, in the Battle for the Atlantic, the Allied navies had the information they needed to locate and destroy the German submarines that had prevented supplies from reaching the British Isles. With the submarines gone, American ships carrying troops and weapons reached Europe safely, and the Allies were able to invade France in June 1944, a step that led to the defeat of Germany. It has been said that the breaking of the Enigma may have shortened the war by two years.

The code-breaking efforts also led to the invention of the first electronic computer. This machine, called the Colossus, was developed to tackle another German cipher machine (called the Lorenz cipher), but it had its roots in the bombe machines that were used to unravel the Enigma.

The breaking of the Enigma cipher is considered one of the greatest intelligence achievements in history. It was kept secret for decades after the war, and when the story was finally made public in 1974, many German mathematicians who had worked with the machine didn't believe that the Allies could have possibly broken their codes. They were *almost* correct—if the German cipher clerks and the submarine captain had followed their security instructions, not even the brightest minds and the fastest machines at Bletchley Park could have conquered the Enigma!

The Enigma in use.

catch you later!

So, did you catch a *code*? Or two or three? Which one was your favorite?

You've got lots of **codes** and **ciphers** in your head right now. Just to name a few, you've got the **dots and dashes** of **Morse code**, the strange symbols of the Pigpen code, the secret vocabulary of double talk, and the shifted alphabets of your **cipher wheel**.

And let's not forget codes that hide words in messages and books. That's the kind of code we're going to leave you with this month. It's the Bookworm Code (from **Operation Bookworm Code** on page 40), and it uses the pages of this very book!

So, figure out this message, and we'll see you next month!

47. 8. 3
22. 8. 13
14. 1. 2
34. 7. 12

SPYquest

(continued from page 15)

You ride your bike extra fast, arriving at the Starlight Café just before three. You walk past and glance in the windows, but you don't see Ms. Lightly inside. You wait on a bench down the street, so you can watch the entrance.

Just then, you see your science teacher, Mr. Shader, coming down the street. He stops outside the café and looks at his watch. What's he doing here? Is this just a coincidence, or is Mr. Shader involved in the secret meeting somehow?

Then you see Ms. Lightly pull up in her car and park outside. She gets out of her car and says hello to Mr. Shader. Then, to your horror, they kiss!

Ms. Lightly and Mr. Shader? Yuck!

You're so busy being shocked and surprised that you don't realize Ms. Lightly is looking right at you.

She says something to Mr. Shader and approaches you.

"How'd you get here after school so fast?" she asks.

You decide to explain everything.

"Well, you know that message on the board," you begin.

"You decoded it, didn't you?" Ms. Lightly says. "I had a feeling you were a code breaker."

"I can't believe it was from Mr. Shader," you say, still in shock, though now it's clear why the handwriting looked so familiar.

She laughs. "We've been dating for a couple of months now, but we wanted to keep it quiet. He came up with the idea of using codes. I hope you can keep our secret."

You tell her you will. She smiles and walks back to the café entrance, where Mr. Shader is waiting. She says something to him, and he looks sternly at you.

So, you solved the mystery and uncovered the secret. But all you can think is, "Ick! How could she ever go out with *him*?"

The end! Quest accomplished!

Yes!

theanswerspot

Page 4 (Loads of Codes!):

"ESUOY HT ML AOOHCR SETFE AT MEEM" : Check out More from Headquarters #2 in **Operation Crack the Scramble** (on page 30).

ATYAHHAJP: Use your skills from **Operation Code Buster**. Find the most common letter, and line up that letter under the E on your cipher wheel. Can you decipher the word now?

Once you've done your decoding, you can check your answers at the bottom of this page!

Page 15 (Operation Quiet Morse):

The mission starts on Monday.

Page 17–18 (Operation Cipher Wheel):

2.a. GJBFWJ TK UFZQF N YMNSP XMJX QN XYJSNSL YT ZX
   b. RJJY RJ FY HMJHPUTNSY FQUMF

3.a. Mr. Brown is not really who he says he is.
   b. Wear a disguise to the meeting.
   c. I will wear a red hat so you will recognize me.

Page 19–20 (Operation Deeper Meaning):

Part 1: You will meet a new contact tomorrow at four.

Part 2: Contact is a double agent.

Page 23 (Operation Double Talk):

a. I'm going to follow someone today.

b. Let's have a meeting after school tomorrow.

Page 25 (Operation Pigpen Code):

a. His bowtie is really a camera.
b. Big brother is watching.
c. Message coming tomorrow.

Page 25 (Spy Quest):

Starlight Wednesday at three.

Page 27 (Operation ADFGX Cipher):

FF XA GF AG XA GX

Code

Meet at dawn.

More from Headquarters #3: Your next mission is in Hollywood.

Page 30 (Operation Crack the Scramble):

1.a. The launch will be at dawn.
   b. Beware of double agent.
   c. You are being followed.
   d. Secret meeting at midnight.

2. To code or not to code, that is the question. (The code uses reverse writing, and the last letter in each word is exchanged with the first letter of the next word.)

Page 32 (Operation Code Buster):

The fault lies not in our stars but in ourselves—Shakespeare

Page 32 (Spy Quest):

Meet me on Wednesday at three.

Page 36 (Operation Cipher Table):

I need help with the next mission.

Page 38–39 (Operation Spy Code):

The first message reads: The bird is out of the cage.

1. a. Expect visit tonight.
   b. Meet me at recess.
   c. Matthew is a spy.

2. a. Beware of Jordan.
   b. Math homework is fun.
   c. Trouble ahead. I need help.

Page 40 (Operation Bookworm Code):

Call Jack Friday at seven.

Page 47 (Catch You Later):

Leave no code unbroken.

Page 4:
Meet me at my house after school. Excellent!